Snapdragons

Stage 10

Gill Howell

KU-338-084

Teaching Notes

Contents

Clown School

Emily and the Lamb

The Sparrow, the Crow and the Pearl

Tom the Whistling Wonder

Prince Albert's Birthday

The Selkie Child

Introduction

The *Snapdragons* series is a rich mix of different kinds of stories presented as picture books with expertly written text carefully levelled to provide reading practice at each stage in Key Stage 1.

The six books at Stage 10 are intended to bridge the transition to Key Stage 2 by providing a wide variety of genre with challenging, extended stories that will encourage children to become confident readers. The stories in this set have a literary dimension with a more sophisticated tone and variety of language. The sustained reading required for these extended stories, with longer and more complex sentence structures, will help develop reading stamina. They also provide further practice in reading key words, develop an understanding of wordplay, and extend the children's vocabulary through specialised terms related to the different contexts.

The books in Stage 10 include stories based in familiar settings featuring personal observations and the senses. In addition, there is a humorous tale set in a royal household, and traditional tales from other cultures.

While following the plot through these longer texts, the children are still encouraged to look at the illustrations for visual cues to the words and to predict what is happening in the story. The picture book presentation will also inspire children to tell the story in their own words so that they develop their oral skills.

How to introduce the books

Before reading the story for guided or independent reading, always read the title and talk about the picture on the cover.

Go through the book together, looking at the pictures and talking about them. If there are context words (listed in the chart on page 4) that are new or unfamiliar, point them out and read them with the children. Read the story to the children, encouraging confident children to join in with you.

This booklet provides prompts and suggestions for using the books in groups and for guided, group and independent activities, matched to text, sentence and word level objectives. There are also separate Guided Reading Cards available for six titles at each stage. Suggestions are also provided for speaking and listening activities, writing activities, and cross-curricular links. You can use these suggestions to follow on from your reading or at another time.

Reading notes are also provided in each book. They can be found on the inside front and back covers of each book. These suggest friendly prompts and activities for parents or carers reading with their children at home.

Reading skills

Stage 10 develops:
- confident, independent reading
- awareness of more complex sentences
- understanding of a wider range of stories, beyond everyday experience
- awareness of more complex plots
- a readiness for conventional text layout
- inferential comprehension skills
- inferring author's intention
- awareness of other viewpoints
- insights into feelings and motives of characters
- consolidation of independent writing skills.

Vocabulary chart

Stage 10		
Clown School	Year 2 High frequency words	about after again an as back be because been but by came could did do door down first from good got had have help her here him his how if jump just last laugh(ed) little made make man much must name next not now off old one or out over people put ran red saw school seen so take that them then there these time too took two very want water way were what when where who will with your
	Context words	bakery balloons cautiously clown complicated costume custard pie enormous explanation persuasively policewoman weight
Emily and the Lamb	Year 2 High frequency words	about again as back ball be because but by called came can't do don't first from good got had half have help her him his home house if just laughed made make more much next not off old one our out over pull put ran saw school sister so some take than that them then there three time too took tree two very want water way were what when where will with would your
	Context words	calves cousins lambs referee Scotland thistles whistle
The Sparrow, the Crow and the Pearl	Year 2 High frequency words	about after again an as back be because but by called came can't could do don't down from good got had have help her here him his house how if jump(ing) just laugh(ed) little lived make man much next not off once one out over put should so that them then there time too took tree two very want way were what when where will with would your
	Context words	argument creature crow elephant embarrassed mosquito pearl sparrow
Tom the Whistling Wonder	Year 2 High frequency words	about again an another back ball be because been but by came can't could do door down first from four got had have help him his home house if jump made now off one our out over push(ed) pull ran should sister so that their then there three too took tree two us water way were what when where who with your
	Context words	anxious cough crow fierce furious stranger swallows warbling whistle
Prince Albert's Birthday	Year 2 High frequency words	another as back be because but by call came could did do don't door down from good has have her him his how if last live made make many more must name new next not now off old once our out over people put ran seen that their then there time too took very water way were what when who will with would your
	Context words	Albert Alice beaver birthday bowler dessert James moustache parlour raspberry royal strawberry Victoria whiskers
The Selkie Child	Year 2 High frequency words	about again as back be bed been but by call(ed) came did down from four had has have her here him his home house how if just laugh(ed) little live lived loved made make more must night now off old once one or out over people saw so some seven take that their them then there three time took us very water way were what when where who with would blue grey white silver
	Context words	crystal daughter deserted driftwood human islands legend mermaids mortal pebbles seal Selkie treasure

Curriculum coverage chart

Stage 10	Speaking and listening	Reading	Writing
Clown School			
NLS/SLL	Y3T1 28	T2, S3, W7, W9	T16
Scotland	Level B	Level B	Level B
N. Ireland	Activities: b, d, e Outcomes: a, b, d, e, f	Activities: a, b, c, e, f, h Outcomes: a, b, h	Outcomes: d, h, i, k
Wales	Range: 1, 2, 4, 5 Skills: 1, 2	Range: 1, 2, 3, 5, 6 Skills: 1, 2, 3, 4, 5, 7, 8	Range: 1, 3, 4, 5 Skills: 1, 5, 6
Emily and the Lamb			
NLS/SLL	Y3T1 26	T3, S3, W11	T10
Scotland	Level B	Level B	Level B
N. Ireland	Activities: a, b, e, f Outcomes: a, b, c, d	Activities: a, b, c, e, f, h Outcomes: a, b, h	Outcomes: a, b, c, d, f, k
Wales	Range: 1, 4 Skills: 1, 2, 5	Range: 1, 2, 3, 5, 6 Skills: 1, 2, 3, 4, 5, 7, 8	Range: 1, 3, 4, 5 Skills: 1, 5, 6
The Sparrow, the Crow and the Pearl			
NLS/SLL	T3/Y3T1 28	T1, S3, W7, W13	T16
Scotland	Level B	Level B	Level B
N. Ireland	Activities: a, b, d Outcomes: b, d, e	Activities: a, b, e, f, g, h, i, j Outcomes: a, h	Outcomes: a, b, d
Wales	Range: 1, 5 Skills: 1, 2	Range: 1, 2, 3, 5, 6 Skills: 1, 2, 3, 4, 5, 7, 8	Range: 1, 3, 4, 5 Skills: 1, 3, 5, 6
Tom the Whistling Wonder			
NLS/SLL	T8/Y3T1 26	T3, S3, W19	T10, T16
Scotland	Level B	Level B	Level B
N. Ireland	Activities: a, e, f Outcomes: a, c, d	Activities: a, b, c, d, e, f, h Outcomes: a, h, i	Outcomes: a, b, c, d, f, k
Wales	Range: 1, 4 Skills: 1, 2, 5, 6, 7	Range: 1, 2, 3, 5, 6 Skills: 1, 2, 3, 4, 5, 7, 8	Range: 1, 3, 4, 5 Skills: 1, 5, 6
Prince Albert's Birthday			
NLS/SLL	Y3T1 26	T3, S3, W13	T10, T16
Scotland	Level B	Level B	Level B
N. Ireland	Activities: a, f Outcomes: a, c, d	Activities: a, b, c, e, f, h, i, j Outcomes: a, h	Outcomes: a, b, c, d, f, k
Wales	Range: 1, 4 Skills: 1, 2, 5, 6, 7	Range: 1, 2, 3, 5, 6 Skills: 1, 2, 3, 4, 5, 7, 8	Range: 1, 3, 4, 5 Skills: 1, 2, 5, 6
The Selkie Child			
NLS/SLL	Y3T1 26	T1, S4, W8	T11
Scotland	Level B	Level B	Level B
N. Ireland	Activities: a, e, f Outcomes: a, c, d	Activities: a, b, c, e, f, h, i, j Outcomes: a, b, h, i	Outcomes: a, b, c, f
Wales	Range: 1, 4 Skills: 1, 5, 6, 7	Range: 1, 2, 3, 5, 6 Skills: 1, 2, 3, 4, 5, 7, 8	Range: 1, 3, 4, 5 Skills: 1, 2, 5, 6

Clown School

Reading the story

Introducing the story

- Look together at the front cover, read the title and the author's name.
- Ask the children what the cover illustration shows, and to suggest where the story is set.
- Ask the children to look through the book briefly, focusing on the illustrations to confirm their ideas.
- Turn to page 3 and ask them to suggest who features in the illustration, and what sort of person they think he will be.

During reading

- Ask the children to read in a quiet voice as you listen to them individually.
- Praise the children when they read with pace and use appropriate strategies to make sense of the text.
- On page 2, ask: *Why is "lots" written in bold print? What effect does this have on the way you read the sentence?*
- Encourage the children as they continue through the story to read the words in bold print with emphasis.
- Where necessary, prompt the children to reread sentences and paragraphs to make sense of their reading.
- Point out the verbs that describe speech, and encourage the children to reread the spoken words with the expression appropriate to the reporting clauses (e.g. p7 "snapped", p8 "ordered", p9 "sighed", "snarled").

Observing Check that the children:
- ■ draw on a range of strategies to make sense of their reading.

Group and independent reading activities

Text level work

Range humorous story/familiar setting

Objective How dialogue is presented in stories, e.g. through statements, questions, exclamations; how paragraphing is used to organise dialogue (T2).

- Ask the children to turn to page 2, and read the dialogue between Roz, Mum and Dad.
- Ask the children: *How is the text written when someone starts speaking?* Point out that the spoken words are indented on a new line for each contributor to the dialogue.
- Encourage the children read page 4. Ask them to find the speech marks that denote the spoken words.
- Ask the children to look at the first paragraph and find the second sentence within speech marks, *"I will be your teacher."* Ask: *Why doesn't this sentence begin on a new line?* (It is the same speaker.)
- Ask the children to look through the text and find other examples of spoken words where a new line <u>is not</u> used, and to look for the reason.

Observing Do the children scan the text for speech marks in order to find dialogue quickly?

Sentence level work

Objective The function of verbs in sentences through: collecting and classifying examples of verbs from reading and own knowledge, e.g. *said, whispered, shrieked* (S3).

- Point out that there are a number of clues an author uses to help readers read dialogue expressively, e.g. question marks, exclamation marks, and italic or bold print.
- Ask the children to suggest other ways in which an author tells readers how words are spoken by characters in stories.
- Encourage the children to look through the story and collect verbs used to describe speech. (said, suggested, announced, declared, growled, explained, replied, snapped, mumbled, ordered, sighed, snarled, asked, cried, grumbled, yelled, informed, shouted, began, answered, laughed)
- Ask the children to read the list of verbs they find, and to say which have similar meanings, e.g. shouted/yelled, announced/declared.
- Ask them to add the verbs to their personal word banks.

Observing Do the children differentiate between verbs in reporting clauses and adverbs, e.g. "she said persuasively"?

Word level work

Objectives To practise new spellings regularly by "Look, say, cover, write, check" strategy (W7); To investigate and learn to use the spelling pattern *le* as in *little, muddle, bottle, scramble, cradle* (W9).

- Ask the children to turn to page 7 and put their fingers on the word "wobbled".
- Point out the present tense of the verb "wobble" and the spelling pattern at the end of the word ("le"), and ask them to scan the text and find other examples of words using the same ending ("-bled"). ("mumbled", "grumbled", "stumbled", "tumbled")
- Ask the children to write the words on their boards using the present tense form, and to practise their spelling, using Look, Cover, Write and Check.

Observing Do the children scan the text to find the words?

Speaking and listening activities

Objective To present events and characters through dialogue to engage the interest of an audience (Y3T1 28).

- Ask the children to say who the two main characters are.
- Ask the children to work with a partner and discuss how to present the interaction between Roz and Mr Bozo as a play for an audience.
- Ask some of the pairs to act out their ideas for the class.

Cross-curricular link
◀▶ Art and Design: design a clown costume

Writing

Objective To begin to organise stories into paragraphs; to begin to use paragraphing in presentation of dialogue in stories (T16).

- Ask the children to think about what Roz would say when she went home again after the end of the story.
- Remind the children of the Text level activity (identifying when dialogue begins on a new indented line).
- Ask the children to write a passage describing a conversation between Roz and her parents about what happened that day at Clown School.

Emily and the Lamb

Reading the story

Introducing the story

- Look together at the front cover, read the title and the author's name.
- Ask the children what the cover illustration shows, and to suggest where the story is set. Let them look through the book briefly, focusing on the illustrations to confirm their ideas.
- Ask the children to read the first sentence of the story. Point out that this story is being told by Emily.
- Ask the children, while they are reading, to think about how Emily feels about the other characters in the story.

During reading

- Ask the children to read in a quiet voice as you listen to them individually.
- Praise the children when they read with pace and use appropriate strategies to make sense of the text.
- On page 3, ask the children to suggest why Emily wishes she were on her own with Gran and Grandad.
- On page 5, ask: *How do you think Claire says "Oh Emily!"? How does Claire feel about Emily? How does Patrick feel about Emily?*
- Encourage the children to read the words spoken by the children on pages 11–12 in a tone of voice that shows how they feel.
- On page 19, ask the children why they think the author has used much shorter sentences than on the previous pages.
- At the end of the story, ask: *How do you think Emily feels now?*

Observing Check that the children:
- understand the relationship between Emily and her older sisters and cousins.

Group and independent reading activities

Text level work

Range familiar setting/story based on observation and senses

Objective To be aware of the different voices in stories using dramatised readings, showing differences between the narrator and different characters used, e.g. puppets to present stories (T3).

- Ask the children to work with a partner. Tell one child to take the role of Emily, and the other to read all the other characters.
- Ask the children to only read the spoken words, and not Emily's narrative.
- Remind the children to read their character's words using a tone of voice appropriate to the character (as if they really were the character).

Observing Do the children scan the text for speech marks in order to find dialogue quickly? Do their tones of voice reflect the relationship between Emily and the other characters?

Sentence level work

Objective The function of verbs in sentences through: experimenting with changing simple verbs in sentences and discussing their impact on meaning (S3).

You will need the following extracts from sentences in the story, written on the board or on paper, with "went" as a substitute for the verbs:

Grandad went up the hill … and I went behind.
We went right up to the top of a high, stony ridge.
I went down the hill and kicked the thistles.

- Ask the children to read the first sentence aloud. Ask: *What does the verb "went" tell us about the hill or the characters?*
- Ask the children to turn to page 8 and find the full text on the page. Ask them to read the sentences with the verbs the author used, and say how it changes the meaning. Ask: *What do the verbs "walked" and "hurried" tell you about the two characters?*
- Ask the children to read the second sentence, and find the full sentence on page 8.
- Ask: *What does the use of the verb "climbed" tell us about the setting?*
- Ask the children to read the third sentence and find the full sentence on page 10.
- Ask: *What does the verb "stomped" tell you about Emily's feelings?*
- Ask the children to suggest why authors use a variety of powerful verbs in stories.

Observing Do the children understand that the use of powerful verbs helps readers build a personal mental picture of character and setting?

Word level work

Objective To use their knowledge of prefixes to generate new words from root words, especially antonyms, *happy/unhappy, appear/disappear* (W11).

- On page 11, ask the children to find what Katie, Claire and Emily say about Emily playing with them. ("not fair")
- Ask the children to suggest another way of saying the opposite of "fair". (unfair)
- Together, brainstorm a list of words that use "un" to create the opposite meaning, e.g. kind, happy, tidy, true, clear.

Observing Do the children test words themselves before suggesting them for the list?

Speaking and listening activities

Objective To follow up others' points and show whether they agree or disagree in a whole-class discussion (Y3T1 26).

- Refer the children to the dialogue in the story on pages 11–13.
- Ask the children to suggest reasons why Emily's cousins and sisters do not want her to join their game, and why Patrick does.
- Ask the children to read pages 22 and 24. *Ask: Do you think Emily's actions will change the way the others treat her?*
- Ask the children to think about a new conversation for the story, between Emily and the other children after the story ending.
- Scribe the children's suggestions on the board for a future writing activity.

Cross-curricular link
◀▶ PSHE: belonging to various groups and communities such as family and school

Writing

Objective Using reading as a model, to write own passages of dialogue (T10).

- Refer the children to the suggestions for a new conversation drawn up previously (see the Speaking and listening activity).
- Ask the children to write a new dialogue between Emily and two of the other children.
- Remind the children how the use of verbs in reporting speech can help readers understand how the words are spoken by the characters.

The Sparrow, the Crow and the Pearl

Reading the story

Introducing the story

- Look together at the front cover, read the title and the author's name.
- Ask the children what the cover illustration shows, and to suggest where the story might be set.
- Encourage the children to look through the book briefly, focusing on the illustrations to confirm their ideas.
- Ask the children, while they are reading, to think about the character of the Sparrow.

During reading

- Ask the children to read in a quiet voice as you listen to them individually.
- Praise the children when they read with pace and use appropriate strategies to make sense of the text.
- On pages 3–4, ask the children to find words that tell them how Sparrow is feeling. Ask: *How has she changed from the first two pages?*
- On page 5, ask the children to find a sentence with a word in italic print, and to read the sentence expressively. Ask: *What does the emphasis on "you" tell us about what Crow thinks?*
- Where necessary, prompt the children to reread sentences and paragraphs to make sense of their reading.
- At the end of the story, ask: *Why do you think Mosquito was the only one to do as Sparrow asked?*

Observing Check that the children:
- ■ draw on a range of strategies to make sense of their reading.

Group and independent reading activities

Text level work

Range traditional story from another culture

Objective To compare a range of story settings, and to select words and phrases that describe scenes (T1).

- Ask the children to think about where the story is set.
- Ask the children to look through the text and find sentences, words and phrases that tell them about the setting. Ask them to write what they find on their whiteboards.
- Ask the children to work with a partner and compare their findings. Ask them to say where most of the story takes place (a garden) and find the page where the setting moves away from the garden (page 16).
- Model how to draw a map of the settings, e.g.

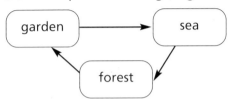

- Ask the children to draw their own map and add words and phrases from the text that describe the settings, e.g. "beautiful garden", "woodcutter's house", "kennel", "shed".

Observing Do the children look through the text to identify the setting, or rely on the illustrations?

Sentence level work

Objective The function of verbs in sentences through: collecting and classifying examples of verbs from reading and own knowledge, e.g. *said, whispered, shrieked* (S3).

- Explain to the children that the ways in which characters speak tell readers about who they are, what they are thinking, and about their personalities.
- Ask the children to look through the story and collect verbs used to describe speech (e.g. "tweeted", "said", "squawked", "cawed", "grumbled").
- Ask the children to work with a partner and compare lists.
- Encourage the children to discuss the meanings of the verbs, and to circle the verbs that tell them about the speaker's feelings.

Observing Do the children differentiate between verbs used that reflect the type of character (e.g. "tweeted", "squawked") and those that express emotion (e.g. "snapped", "sighed").

Word level work

Objectives To practise new spellings regularly by "look, say, cover, write, check" strategy (W7); To collect new words from reading and work in other subjects and create ways of categorising and logging them, e.g. personal dictionaries, glossaries (W13).

- Ask the children to refer to the list of verbs collected in the Sentence level activity (see above).
- Let the children add any new verbs used to describe speech to their personal word banks.
- Ask the children to practise their spelling using Look, Cover, Write and Check.

Observing Do the children scan their lists by initial letter to add them in alphabetical order?

Speaking and listening activities

Objectives To be aware of different voices in stories using dramatised readings, showing differences between the narrator and different characters used (T3); To present events and characters through dialogue to engage the interest of an audience (Y3T1 28).

You will need stick puppets

- Ask the children to work in small groups, and provide them with stick puppets of Sparrow, Crow, Tree, Woodcutter, Mouse, Dog, Stick, Fire, Sea, Elephant, Mosquito.
- Ask one child to take the role of Sparrow, and get the rest of the group to share the other characters.
- Encourage the children to act out the story using the stick puppets.
- Ask some groups to perform their dramatisation for the class.

Cross-curricular link
◀▶ Art and Design: design and make stick puppets

Writing

Objective To begin to organise stories into paragraphs (T16).

- Ask the children to refer to the maps they drew in the Text level activity, and to write a paragraph describing each setting. Encourage them to use the notes from their maps, and their own imaginings.

Tom the Whistling Wonder

Reading the story

Introducing the story

- Look together at the front cover, read the title and the author's name.
- Ask the children to turn to pages 2–3, and identify the characters in the illustration, and find their names in the text.
- Ask the children to suggest what the story will be about.
- Let the children look through the book briefly, focusing on the illustrations to confirm their ideas.

During reading

- Ask the children to read in a quiet voice as you listen to them individually.
- Praise the children when they read with pace and use appropriate strategies to make sense of the text.
- On page 5, ask the children to suggest why the author uses "demanded" instead of "asked". Ask: *Are the three bigger children being friendly to Tom?*
- Remind the children to read the spoken words with an expressive tone.
- On page 15, ask: *Why do you think Tom had gone to climb the tree already?*
- At the end of the story, ask: *Do you think this is a serious story? What did you find funny in it?*

Observing Check that the children:
- recognise the figurative language in the story, e.g. "monster dog", "like a wild bird", "out-of-the-blue birdsong".

Group and independent reading activities

Text level work

Range familiar setting/story based on observation and senses

Objective To be aware of the different voices in stories using dramatised readings, showing differences between the narrator and different characters used, e.g. puppets to present stories (T3).

- Ask the children, in groups of four, to each take the role of a character from the story, and read all the dialogue.
- Remind the children to only read the spoken words, and not the narrative.
- Remind the children to read their character's words using a tone of voice appropriate to the character.

Observing Do the children scan the text for speech marks in order to find dialogue quickly? Do their tones of voice reflect the humour in the hierarchy of their relationships?

Sentence level work

Objective The function of verbs in sentences through: collecting and classifying examples of verbs from reading and own knowledge, e.g. *said, whispered, shrieked*; experimenting with changing simple verbs in sentences and discussing their impact on meaning (S3).

You will need the following sentences from the story written on the board or paper.

"I spy a stranger," Danny said.
"Can I play?" asked Tom.
"What now?" asked Melody.

- Ask the children to read the first sentence aloud. Ask: *What does the verb "said" tell us about how Danny says the words?*
- Ask the children to think how the meaning would change if the verb describing the speech was changed. Change the verb to "whispered" and ask if this affects the sentence.
- Draw up a list of verbs used in the story and, from the children's prior experience, verbs that could be used as a replacement for "said" and "asked", e.g. demanded, exclaimed, moaned, whined, pleaded.
- Ask the children to work with a partner and change the verbs to alternatives, reading them aloud and discussing how the effect or tone of voice is altered.
- Ask the children to suggest why authors use a variety of powerful verbs in stories.

Observing Do the children understand that the use of powerful verbs helps readers build a personal mental picture of characters and what they are thinking?

Word level work

Objective Common vocabulary for introducing and concluding dialogue, e.g. *said, replied, asked*. Collect examples from reading (W19).

- Ask the children to scan the text and collect the examples of verbs used to describe dialogue.
- Ask them to add other verbs from their own knowledge.
- Let the children add these to their personal word lists.

Observing Do the children scan the text for speech punctuation to identify dialogue?

Speaking and listening activities

Objectives To express their views about a story or poem, identifying specific words and phrases to support their viewpoint (T8); To follow up others' points and show whether they agree or disagree in a whole-class discussion (Y3T1 26).

- Write "sad, funny, exciting, frightening, mysterious" on the board.
- Ask the children which word, or words, best describes the story.
- From the children's suggestions, scribe two sentences to describe what kind of story it is. Hold a class vote on which sentence they think is the most accurate.

Cross-curricular link
◀▶ PSHE: take part in discussions with one person and the whole class

Writing

Objectives Using reading as a model, to write own passages of dialogue (T10); To begin to organise stories into paragraphs; to begin to use paragraphing in presentation of dialogue in stories (T16).

- Look together at page 4. Remind the children how a new person's spoken words are written on a new line.
- Ask the children to think about how they would act if a new person came and asked if they could join in their games.
- Model how to open the story using the children's suggestions, e.g. John and I were playing on our skateboards in the park. Suddenly a girl came up to us. "Can I play?" she asked... .
- Ask the children to write two paragraphs about a new child asking to play with them.

Prince Albert's Birthday

Reading the story

Introducing the story

- Look together at the front cover, read the title and the author's name.
- Ask the children what the cover illustration shows, and ask them to suggest when the story is set. (It is an historical story set in Victorian times.)
- Ask the children to suggest what the story will be about.
- Ask them to look through the book briefly, focusing on the illustrations to confirm their ideas.
- Identify any new or unusual words before reading the story, e.g. "gracious" (p4), "banquet" (p10), "enclosure" (p20).

During reading

- Ask the children to read in a quiet voice as you listen to them individually.
- Praise the children when they read with pace and use appropriate strategies to make sense of the text.
- On pages 2–3, ask the children to think about how a queen would speak to a servant and encourage them to read the conversation between Queen Victoria and James the butler in an expressive tone of voice.
- On page 9, ask the children to suggest what "spiffing" means. Ask them to say why the author has used this word instead of a more modern alternative.
- On page 16, ask: *Why do you think Queen Victoria fainted?*
- On page 18, ask the children what "keep a stiff upper lip" means. Ask: *Does the Queen really want Alice to make her top lip stiff?*
- On page 24, ask them what they think James has gone to find.
- Where necessary, prompt the children to reread sentences and paragraphs to make sense of their reading.
- At the end of the story, ask: *Do you think this is a serious story? What did you find funny or serious in it?*

Observing Check that the children:
- read Queen Victoria's words in an appropriately formal tone of voice.

Group and independent reading activities

Text level work

Range humorous story/language play

Objective To be aware of the different voices in stories using dramatised readings, showing differences between the narrator and different characters used, e.g. puppets to present stories (T3).

- Ask the children to work with a partner, and take turns to read the spoken words in the story.
- Remind the children to read their character's words using a voice appropriate to the character (as if they really were the character).

Observing Do the children scan the text for speech marks in order to find dialogue quickly? Do they alter their tone for each character?

Sentence level work

Objective The function of verbs in sentences through: collecting and classifying examples of verbs from reading and own knowledge, e.g. *said, whispered, shrieked* (S3).

- Ask the children to turn to page 3 and find the verb phrase "said loudly".
- Encourage the children to suggest another verb that could replace the phrase, e.g. shouted, yelled, cried.
- Ask: *Why do you think the author uses the verb phrase?*
- Ask the children to scan the text and find other verbs that are used instead of "said".
- Get the children to add new verbs to their personal word banks.

Observing Do the children understand the dignity and formal nature of the way the Queen speaks?

Word level work

Objective To collect new words from reading and work in other subjects and create ways of categorising and logging them, e.g. personal dictionaries, glossaries (W13).

- Discuss how the story is set in Victorian times.
- Ask the children to look through the text and find any words or phrases that they think are no longer common today (e.g. "trifle heavy", "how amusing", "spiffing", "parlour").

- Ask the children to suggest how they would say the same thing today.
- Let the children add the words and phrases to their personal word banks.

Observing Do the children recognise that the use of language is appropriate to the setting of the story?

Speaking and listening activities

Objective To follow up others' points and show whether they agree or disagree in a whole-class discussion (Y3T1 26).

- Ask the children to think about why Queen Victoria wanted a beaver hat for Prince Albert, and to find the evidence in the text.
- Ask the children to give an opinion about using animal skin to make clothing.
- Draw up a list of points for and against.
- Hold a class vote.

Cross-curricular link
◀▶ History: identify differences between ways of life at different times (Victorian times)

Writing

Objectives Using reading as a model, to write own passages of dialogue (T10); To begin to organise stories into paragraphs; to begin to use paragraphing in presentation of dialogue in stories (T16).

- Ask the children to suggest what might happen if James returned with a bowler from a cricket team, instead of a bowler hat.
- Ask the children to imagine what the Queen would say, and to write an imagined conversation between the Queen and James.
- Remind the children to begin each person's spoken words on a new line, and to use verbs and verb phrases to describe their words.

The Selkie Child
Reading the story

Introducing the story

- Look together at the front cover, read the title and the author's name.
- Ask the children what the cover illustration shows, and ask them to suggest where the story is set.
- Together, read pages 2–3, and ask the children what they think the story will be about.
- Ask the children to look through the book briefly, focusing on the illustrations to confirm their ideas.

During reading

- Ask the children to read in a quiet voice as you listen to them individually.
- Praise the children when they read with pace and use appropriate strategies to make sense of the text.
- On page 3, ask the children what they understand by the words "haunting beauty".
- On pages 8–9, point out the phrases "swirled in a fury" and "turned to silver". Ask the children if these are literal or figurative phrases. Ask: Are *these words used to mean exactly what they say, or to give an image to readers?*
- On page 15, ask: *Why did laughter and song leave the house?*
- On page 17, check the children understand the meaning of "mortal".
- On page 18, ensure the children understand their reading. Ask: *Why do you think Morgan's eyes light up when she hears the seals?*
- Where necessary, prompt the children to reread sentences and paragraphs to make sense of their reading.
- On page 23, ask the children what they think "Seven tears for seven children" will mean.
- Ask: *Why was the Selkie King kind to Kate and John at the end of the story?*

Observing Check that the children:
  - read high frequency words with pace and confidence, and make sense of the story.

Group and independent reading activities

Text level work

Range legend/story based on observation and senses

Objective To compare a range of story settings, and to select words and phrases that describe scenes (T1).

- Ask the children to read the first two sentences on page 4.
- Explain that the author, in these two sentences, has given readers a brief, direct description of the setting.
- Ask the children to imagine that they are in the place where the story is set. Ask: *What can you see, feel, hear or smell?*
- Ask the children to suggest other details about the setting in their own words.
- Ask the children to work with a partner and look through the story to find other details of the setting in the text. Encourage them to collect words, phrases and sentences.
- Together, discuss the children's findings. Ask: *Does the author give direct descriptions, e.g. "The shore had driftwood and pebbles on it", or are details built up when describing characters' actions, e.g. "Kate … walking among the pebbles and driftwood" (p5).*

Observing Do the children find words from the text, or include description based on the illustrations?

Sentence level work

Objective To use verb tenses with increasing accuracy in speaking and writing, e.g. *catch/caught, see/saw, go/went.* Use past tense consistently for narration (S4).

You will need the following verbs from the story written on the board or paper in the present tense: tell, go, stand, grow, feel, blow, come, see, draw, bend, hide, hold.

- Ask the children to write the verbs in a list.
- Encourage the children to look through the text and find sentences that use these verbs in the past tense.
- Ask the children to write the past tense verb next to the present tense on their lists.
- Let the children practise their spelling, using Look, Cover, Say, Write and Check.

Observing Do the children recognise the irregular forms of past tense verbs?

Word level work

Objective How the spellings of verbs alter when *–ing* is added (W8).

- Ask the children to turn to pages 4–5 and find the following verbs in the text: lived, crouched, baked, loved, went, cleaned, stood, gazed, passed, grew.
- Demonstrate how to write the verb "lived" in its present tense form ("live") and then how to change it to "living".
- Ask the children to write the verbs in a list, and then to write the present tense form next to them, and then to add "–ing".

Observing Do the children understand when to omit the final "e"? Do they recognise the irregular past tense forms of the verbs "go", "stand" and "grow"?

Speaking and listening activities

Objective To follow up others' points and show whether they agree or disagree in a whole-class discussion (Y3T1 26).

- Discuss the legend of the Selkies with the children.
- Ask the children if they believe the legend and why.

Cross-curricular link
◄► PSHE: take part in discussions with one person and the whole class

Writing

Objective To develop the use of settings in own stories by: writing short descriptions of known places; writing a description in the style of a familiar story (T11).

- Remind the children about the Text level activity in which they found words and phrases in the text that described the setting of the story.
- Ask the children to imagine they are one of Kate and John's children. Discuss what they might see, hear, feel and smell.
- Encourage the children to write a short description of walking from the house to the sea, based on their reading and their imagination.

Oxford Reading Tree resources at this level

There is a range of material available at a similar level to these stories which can be used for consolidation or extension.

Stage 10

Teacher support
• Take-Home Card for each story

Further reading
• Robins Packs 1, 2 and 3 at Stages 6–10
• Jackdaws Anthologies Packs 1, 2 and 3 at Stages 8–11
• Glow-worms Poetry Stages 10–11, 11
• Cross-curricular Jackdaws Stages 10–11
• Citizenship Stories Stages 9–10
• True Stories Stages 8–11
• Fact Finders at Stage 10–11
• Treetops Stage 10 upwards
• Branch Library:
> Oxford Reds Narrative Non-fiction Stages 8–10
> What's Their Story? Biographies Packs A and B Stages 10–13

Electronic
• ORT Online www.OxfordReadingTree.com

OXFORD
UNIVERSITY PRESS

Great Clarendon Street, Oxford OX2 6DP

Oxford University Press is a department of the University of Oxford. It furthers the University's objective of excellence in research, scholarship, and education by publishing worldwide in

Oxford   New York

Auckland   Cape Town   Dar es Salaam   Hong Kong   Karachi
Kuala Lumpur   Madrid   Melbourne   Mexico City   Nairobi
New Delhi   Shanghai   Taipei   Toronto

With offices in

Argentina   Austria   Brazil   Chile   Czech Republic   France   Greece
Guatemala   Hungary   Italy   Japan   Poland   Portugal   Singapore
South Korea   Switzerland   Thailand   Turkey   Ukraine   Vietnam

Oxford is a registered trade mark of Oxford University Press
in the UK and in certain other countries

© Oxford University Press 2005

The moral rights of the author have been asserted

Database right Oxford University Press (maker)

First published 2005

British Library Cataloguing in Publication Data

Data available

Series adviser Shirley Bickler

Cover illustration Beccy Blake

Teacher's Notes: ISBN 978-0-19-845585-1

10 9

Page make-up by Fakenham Photosetting, Fakenham, Norfolk

Printed in China by Imago